Where Lost Things Go

Hannah Gradowski

Presentation by *BookLeaf Publishing*

Web: www.bookleafpub.com

E-mail: info@bookleafpub.com

ISBN: 9789358317435

First edition 2023

To those still searching,

*may what you find be better than what was
lost*

ACKNOWLEDGEMENT

I would like to acknowledge that when I said to my partner "I am starting a new project", he did not discourage me... although I already had too much on my plate. Since we have been together, he has often encouraged me to write again even though my passions had been dimmed for several years. I used to write so angrily and in a voice I no longer know now. It took some time to rediscover an old love with the inspiration of a new one. But, our relationship revealed a new voice, emotions, and light. He does not know that he contributes to my writing. Because of him, I am happy and very much in love... and inspired. All of the moments I discuss have led to him. And to God, all I can say is I am so grateful.

When searching for lost things, I found him.

PREFACE

It has been five months since I left my classroom, but I still visit it in dreams and teach as if I was prepared to. When my parents sold my childhood home a year ago, it was the same. I visited it in dreams for a year, knowing it was no longer mine, but a place I felt safe in. It still hurts me to know that I cannot walk into the house that I had grown up in; it hurts me to know that I walked away from the classroom I had begun my career in.

Sometimes, I dream of places more than I dream of people. Perhaps, it is a space to think clearly in or a place that held me in a time of my life that I had felt better in. My apartment now feels like four walls with disarranged spackle from the last resident. It wants to feel like home, but most days it doesn't.

I had moved 2,000 miles away from my hometown to a big city. Sometimes I think about moving back. I know it does not mean that I had failed here, but that I lost more things than found what I was looking for. I watch my parents' age through my cell phone screen and wonder how I could be so selfish for making my life about me. My brothers had moved away too but they came back. I never understood why. Now I do.

My phone calls have been brief lately. It is hard to have a conversation when all they do is end in goodbye. I miss having the company of my family and their contagious laughter echo off one another. My dad celebrated his birthday last week, and I am missing it for the second year in a row. You could not tell me three years ago that this would be the life that I would choose, but it has become a life I could not dream of, nor beg anyone for.

It is lonely to start somewhere new. But dear reader, writing is the same.

People talk about the things you will gain, but do not mention what you will lose. No one mentions that it can be pieces of you.

Childhood home

Tonight, I softly weep
as I visit my childhood house
sound asleep.

It is empty now, abandoned
but the fragrance of our family remains

And it feels so familiar
even though nothing is the same

I am once again wrapped
in its loving embrace
as my fingers graze my favorite places

Each nail scrapes the walls' weathered paint
and each tip unravels frayed threads
in the carpet's seams

Over each doorknob my hands glaze over,
there are doorways
to old stories and memories

And they still feel so real and
so well captured
like recent documentaries

It overwhelms me,
and the house echoes
as I scream.

"You are the only place I've known!"
"Would you even recognize me if I came
home?"

Petoskey stones

My dad takes me treasure hunting
every Tuesday afternoon
and I disappear by the lake's shore
searching for pieces of stone,
searching for more than quarters
a part of lost beach decor.

The waves toss fragments of rocks
as my dad unearths man made jewels.
I wonder if there is even a difference
in value.

He tells me part of the thrill
is in the hunt, but
I used to pick up every stone
Lake Michigan would throw my way.
each one held such a beauty
that I never wanted to cast back away.

Such a foolish girl I was to think I was a house
for many stones,
my shelves became overwhelmed with ones
I could never quite fit right in my heart and
home.

But there has always been one I have been
seeking to find,
the one who is
a treasure of a lifetime.

It is deep beneath waters, and slowly caresses
the shifting floors,
not quite lost, but not quite found
as it lays gently for the one whom it is bound.

I await each Tuesday for its presence on the
shore,
I await to hold it every week, more and more.

It is the thrill of the hunt,
my dad would always say.
I ask, but what if it is worlds away?

He answers.

It will appear when you're most ready for it,
one day.

Prom dress

The final let go, my mother called it.

One, I had once felt so beautiful in
with the soft fabric draped against my skin.

Once, I had loved it obsessively until
I was left tangled in its lace,
my emotions, and remnants of him.

Three years later and
the gown would hauntingly be
behind my closet doors,
like a skeleton figure
hidden by me.

It was another goodbye
my hands did not want to know
as they trembled and clutched
the tailor-made design of black and
gold.

My mother's fingers cradled mine,
releasing the ribbon from nostalgic palms,
freeing the past from my last grip.

She tied the corset delicately, sealing its
Goodbye and
I admired my prom dress for the last time.

The final let go, I called it.

For it cannot be stored in a memory box,
only to be donated and mourned.

The girl it once fit, I have outgrown.

Apocalyptic anxiety

If the world ends tomorrow
And the day ceases to persist

Know that I have no sorrow
If the world ends tomorrow

I will not ask for another day to borrow
For we both did once exist

If the world ends tomorrow
And the day ceases to persist.

Unidentified weapon

She washes her hands a lot
for someone who has never
committed a crime.

But still, she sees the
stains of red from
blood trickle down
each palm of her hand.

and spill over her body.

Still, she washes them
over
and
over
again.

For shame has clung to her
for years
but it is the only
evidence that is left

Of her agony,
and what was taken.

How can anyone believe
that it was theft?

Why is she a sinner
imprisoned in the mind?

Why should she serve the sentence
if she did not commit the crime?

She keeps washing, but does not feel like
she will ever be
clean.

I wonder if they would believe
someone who has been silently
mourning for over
a century.

Ice cream social

My best friend and I chat over Tiny's ice cream
and crowing chickens,
wondering if our small, midwestern hearts
could move to a big city.

With love for the farmland,
we are captured by sunsets,
loud music,
and long drives, but wonder
if city lights can compare to our
shared starry night skies.

We laugh over the meaningless,
proclaiming new gossip as if we were
newspapers in town.
I tell her we will never grow up,
she swears we will never let each other down.

Somedays, I think it is all true
that midwest living can absolutely
create the best in you
but then my eyes wander and I begin to explore
wondering if there is something two-thousand
miles away,
wondering if there's more.

It is constantly on my mind, and I worry because
I cannot stop time,
nor rewind to these parts
when this becomes the past

I am anxious that this may be the last year
we experience everything we have grown to
know
it may be the last time I hear roosters crow
and think of anything but

This being home.

Antiques

There is an Antique Market on North Water
Street,
we used to frequently roam.

Every weekend, we would go when you visited
the city,
a place we called our home.

Inside sat stories on shelves, we would
graze with dusty fingertips and anxiously read,
and write our own
in the aisles of the store's ancient mysteries.

But like the spines of old books, we cracked and
broke
with time.

I tried to hold us bound together but your visits
became sparse and your repeating excuses were
weekly on the dime.

I often wondered when we would meet
in the Antique Market on North Water Street.

For I looked at you then with a future, unaware

we were destined to stay in the past.
I looked at you with the hope that like antiques,
we were built to last.

But eventually, we became another story
in the window's glass,
that other people, just like us,
now walk pass.

Traffic signs

In fleeting crowds of unfamiliar faces,
our eyes met – one finding the other's hue.
in bustling foreign traffic places,
beneath speckled brown and black, I found you.

In stoplight motion constantly red and green,
I held my gaze with you, separating us
from the distant sounds of the city's scene,
hoping for more than the noise to discuss.

But in the commotion of the city's glow,
I did not mean to stare, only to pass through.
but as gold flicked with caution to go,
beneath hurried lights and cars, I lost you.

If only he could have read between my lines,
If only we could have ignored the traffic signs.

The departure

I have lost love once before.
Was it to death or another?

I am sure the feeling is the same.

Watered down writing

I swear I am passionate;
please don't write me off yet.

I know I haven't picked up a pen in ages,
or sat down at my computer for long.

It starts to feel complicated when my writing
asks where I've been and I do not respond.

They ask about the
passions that harbor within me
but it feels like a threat

Some days I feel inspired by their light
and other days, it is every past emotion
I try to ignore and forget.

I do not know if I am good at anything
but being the worst.

I do not know if that makes me talented
in writing,

Or eternally cursed.

Barren arms

What if the child does not come to me
when I call?

For I worry as she wanders.
She is everything, but also
So small.

She whispers to me
in poetry
as I look for her in the clouds

I open my arms widely, but lose
her little face among angel crowds

I ask her to come here
but her tiny feet carry her
away from me
And it is anxiety
I start to feel.

I am breathless as
she runs around
on her own whim

I laugh because

she looks like me, but she acts
like him.

I call again, hearing giggles
of thunder and
imagine her hazel eyes
glisten,

I shout to her loudly
"Come home"
but she does not listen.

What if she does not come to me
when I call?

What if I do not become a mother at all?

Old friends

I think you see a change in yourself
when you start to wish others well
that you used to wish for the worst.

Or when you realize
they are learning to live as you are, and
their mistakes do not mean they need
to be cursed.

Lately, I visit my own
in a living cemetery
and mourn the lives I knew
long ago.

I weep gently at who I was,
and now what I know.

I rehearse my apologies before
greeting each gravestone
with an old friend's name

When I arrive,
I ask for forgiveness from each of them,
and my God
and ask for Him to forgive them the same.

I think you see a change in yourself
when you hope their life is happier
without you around.

Because we are strangers, I hope in life
it is peace that you have found.

Mother's necklace

I will never know her. But when
he is in my arms, I do.

In silence, my hands cradle
his head as if it's his
heart.

And I try to fill the absence of a mother,
but know she will always be a missing
part.

Sometimes I hold him and
wish she knew that
for some, a mother-in-law is a burden,
but for me, it would have been a dream
come true.

Instead, I carry her every day.
in shape of a gold necklace,
an old belonging of hers,

Now, hung on my skin
on display.

Him and I

sit in the stillness
and pray.

I do not know her. But I
feel her around me and
imagine as if she sits here
too.

When her son leans into me
in remembrance,
our eyes fill
with tears to the brim.

I silently talk to her.
I tell her I love him.

Handwritten plans

A year or two ago, I wrote a list of the things
I wanted to see in my life, and how badly
I dreamed for those things to become.

I kept them neat and secure,
I held onto them
With closed hands.

I thought them to be knit tightly
Or sown together and so well planned.

But overtime, my fingers
Unravelled and surprisingly,
I had found myself in love!

With excitement, my hands shook!
And tumbled the plans I had all of
My life.

He kissed my opened palms
And planted new dreams
That I gazed at in anticipation

I had a new list in mind,
New aspirations!

Overtime, our list grew in our
Joined hands
More than before.

Now we long for two little hands
More and more.

God's grace

When your arms are wrapped around my waist,
and my shoulder becomes a home for your head,

I pray for you.

You feel it tickle as
I press my face at the side of your ear.

But I am whispering sweet sayings of safety
to protect you, my dear.

As we hold each other, I feel it
as a heavenly embrace

Some call it love.
I call it being in God's grace.

Season change

It is not as cold as it could be,
but they wear jackets around me.

Maybe I am not used to the change
in weather,

Maybe my body still doesn't feel like
it belongs.

Maybe they are right, maybe I am wrong.

It is not as cold as it could be,

but still, jackets surround me.

Grocery lists

I was alone with a grocery list

A single quart of milk
one dozen eggs
a loaf of bread
a TV dinner
and a bag of coffee

To keep me warm on lonely mornings.

Weekly, I ordered unfulfilling things
Filling my pantry and fridge and storage space

With chocolate, blueberry muffins, and uneaten
cheesecake,
indulgences I did not need,
but wanted anyway.

No one ever tells you that filling voids can be
costly,
especially when they are a temporary fix

And often not too satisfying.

This went on for several months.

Until I met you.

A quart of milk became a gallon.
I added an extra toothbrush, just in case.
A dozen eggs were now two, and
I fell even more for you.

From TV dinners to me learning how to cook,
it was a new adventure that scared me,

But for you, it was worth buying every
cookbook.

I added veggies, protein shakes, granola bars,
and Gatorade and learned to love more than just
the food we made.

It was the time we spent together,
and the messes that covered the counters and the
floors.

It was the lazy pile of dishes, and the
homecooked meal-stench house.
It was the loud burps near midnight, and the
satisfied belly pouches.

Now, you cook for me before I go to work,
and I kiss you goodbye with coffee-stained lips.

I wonder how I ever ate alone before.

I look back at old grocery lists now
and see the amount I supposedly saved,
but in the new receipts,
I find joy in every price that we pay.

Tears in my twenties

I cry over little things easily,
and when it happens in front of you,
I feel like it is a chore, another thing
you have to take care of
before you go to bed.

And I cannot help it, and you have learned
that the tears come out easily,
and sometimes without warning.

But you surprise me
by catching them gently,
or greeting them with your hand
upon my face.

You welcome them when they do not feel
invited,
or when they feel all over the place.

I apologize profusely because they are
unwanted guests that appear too often
in our home.

I tell you that you do not have to take care
of a mess that you were not part of.

You tell me I do not have to be alone.

It is a weird feeling,
to cry and hurt and
to cry and heal.

This is a love I have never known.

Spring cleaning

I wish I could make a nest out of your arms
and crawl deep within your rib cage,
placing a welcome mat
on the front porch of your heart.

I would open the curtains
of your intestines and
dust cob webs away.

I would plant roses, and daises
and sunflowers in
the pits of your stomach and
pluck a few for the table.

I would power wash the
outlining of your organs
and hose down
the dirt and grime.

I would landscape
on the surface of your heart
and bury seeds in your veins.

After a day's work,
I would curl up in the chair of your being,
with a love story in hand,
waiting for you to arrive home to me again.

Vows

My dad spoke to my mom
in her wedding gown.

When he said "I do", he said
I do not want to be with anyone else.

For I could live with anyone in this world,
But it is you, I cannot live without.

He tells me when it is love, you will know.
The emotion cannot be written down.

Hannah's prayer

When I am anxious,
my mother tells me
to pray.

Lord,
thank you for my
mother,
who always knows
what to say.